Dr. Nakeisha Maharaj
Email: NAKEISHA25@YAHOO.COM

Foreword

This book is simply a masterpiece. It teaches young children how to manage money, something most do not understand and many refuse to understand. I want to congratulate Dr. Nakeisha Maharaj on this book. Her concepts were so creatively put together with thoughts that only a caring mother could express. Please get a copy as it will teach your child the vital principles in this book. Children can have fun while learning and this book is able to keep the child's interest while teaching a valuable life lesson.

Dr Dexter James
The Wealth Ambassador

One late afternoon, Jzodha was playing with a broom outside.

Sweeping back and forth when suddenly the broom swept over a bump. "Ouch!!!" it said. Jzodha suddenly dropped the broom and asked in a soft shaky voice, "Who said that?" "Hellooo, a bit of help down here," the voice answered back.

Jzodha slowly stooped down to take a peek, and quickly dug a dollar bill out of the dirt.

"Ugh!! I was not created for this," said the dollar bill as he blew dust off himself.
"Yo.....you.....you can talk?" Jzodha stuttered in amazement.

"Oh yes, I'm Dollarz, What's your name?"

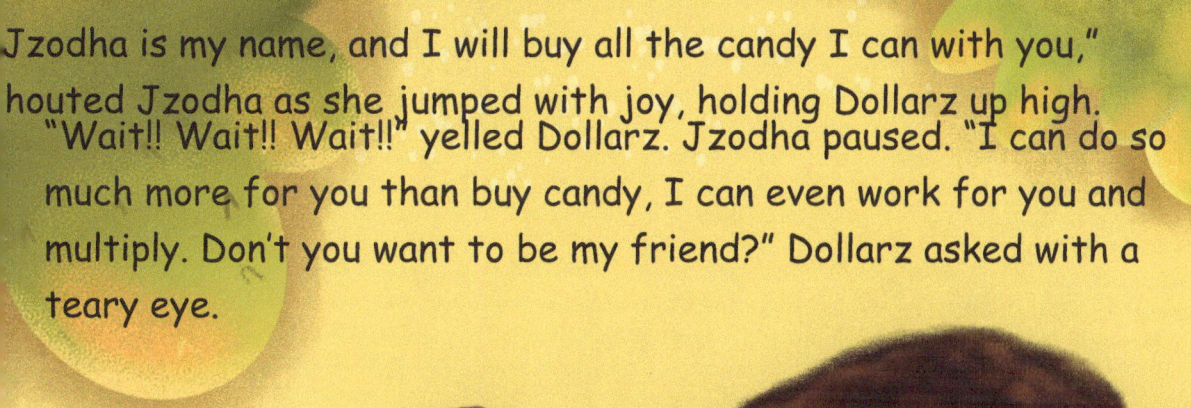

Jzodha is my name, and I will buy all the candy I can with you," shouted Jzodha as she jumped with joy, holding Dollarz up high. "Wait!! Wait!! Wait!!" yelled Dollarz. Jzodha paused. "I can do so much more for you than buy candy, I can even work for you and multiply. Don't you want to be my friend?" Dollarz asked with a teary eye.

"Work for me? That's just silly. I'm only 7 years old." Jzodha responded with laughter.

"Please, please, please keep me for a night., I promise to be good to you if you are good to me," Dollarz replied.

That evening, Jzodha took Dollarz inside the house. It was almost time for supper. As she ran to the bathroom to wash her hands, she put Dollarz on the sink. Suddenly, she got distracted by the sound of her dog RoRo playfully barking, "Ruff! Ruff!"

"Ok RoRo, let's go eat," said Jzodha as
she picked up RoRo and ran off with him, leaving Dollarz
behind. As Dollarz attempted to get Jzodha's attention,
he tripped and fell over in the trash bin.
"Help! Help!" Dollarz cried out but no one could hear him.

Next morning, Jzodha came into the bathroom to brush her teeth.

She spotted the legs of Dollarz hanging out of the trash bin, and she quickly pulled him out.

"Oh no! Sorry Dollarz, from now on I pinky dinky promise to take better care of you." Jzodha said. "I forgive you, no more pulling me out of the dirt and stinky trash bins. If you promise to be my friend, I will help you share love with others, buy candy and help you get more of me, deal?" Dollarz asked. They both agreed and shook hands smiling.

That night they mapped out a plan on paper and gathered things they needed to start. "We will call it the 1-2-3-4 rule." Dollarz suggested.

"What's that?" Jzodha asked. "Let's just say that's how I will help you get more friends like me," winked Dollarz.

"Goodnight Dollarz," said Jzodha with a yawn. "Goodnight Jzodha," Dollarz responded.

Next morning Dollarz was so excited to share his knowledge with Jzodha that he woke her up at 6 am. "It's Saturday, let's paint some pictures," said Dollarz.

"I love painting," responded Jzodha. They painted beautiful pictures with decorative edges until all the painting was finished.

Dollarz insisted that they should go outside with the paintings and hang them on the fence. Jzodha asked her big brother to help her when suddenly, cars slow down and parents asked if the paintings were for sale. Dollarz whispered, "Say yes, say yes, five dollars ($5)." Jzodha said yes and all 15 of her paintings sold.

That night Dollarz said, "I am proud of you, Jzodha. You used items you had, painted pictures you love, and created masterpieces to brighten smiles on others. It's time for a special treat." Oh how Jzodha loved getting special treats.

"Remember our 1-2-3-4 rule, for every dollar you got today we will put 10 cents in our giving bag because it is always better to give something than to receive. Twenty cents (20c) will go in our invest bag to buy more paint.

Thirty cents (30c) will go in your spend bag to buy you candy and other treats and forty cents (40c) will go in the save bag to help you never run out of more of me." Dollarz instructed. "Dollarz I am glad you are my friend." Jzodha said hugging Dollarz.

Next morning it was Jzodha's favorite day of the week, Sunday. She loved wearing dresses. She was up early excited to go to church with her brother. She already knew she wanted to use the money in her giving bag to give to the people at the church who fed the kids that don't have food to eat. This brought more joy to her than buying all the candy in the world.

After church, Jzodha and her brother were walking back home talking about ways they can fill the giving bag with more money when she spotted legs in the grass. It was more money she rescued. "You see Jzodha, we will always follow people that treat us good and share us with love,"". Dollarz said. From this day forward, Jzodha started thinking about ways she could fill each of her bags. She continued giving and giving until more money found their way to her.

You too can become an entrepreneur!

Giving back is fun!

Activity saving jar

All the money I received

	Monday	Tuesday	Wednesday
Week 1			
Week 2			
Week 3			
Week 4			

Monthly Chart

Thursday	Friday	Saturday	Sunday

All the money I spent

	Monday	Tuesday	Wednesday
Week 1			
Week 2			
Week 3			
Week 4			

Monthly Chart

Thursday	Friday	Saturday	Sunday

Thank you for taking the time to read this book. I hope it inspired you to dream big and build confidence to become the next young entrepreneur. Feel free to send us your feedback and let us know how this book has been a blessing to you.

Dr. Nakeisha Maharaj